NFC WEST

BY ELLEN LABRECQUE

★ Arizona Cardinals ★ San Francisco 49ers ★ Seattle Seahawks ★ St. Louis Rams ★

Published by The Child's World®
1980 Lookout Drive
Mankato, MN 56003-1705
800-599-READ
www.childsworld.com

The Child's World®: Mary Berendes, Publishing Director
The Design Lab: Kathleen Petelinsek, Design
Editorial Directions, Inc.: Pam Mamsch and E. Russell Primm,
Project Managers

Photographs ©: Robbins Photography

Library of Congress Cataloging-in-Publication Data
Labrecque, Ellen.
  NFC West / by Ellen Labrecque.
     p. cm. Includes bibliographical references and index.
  ISBN 978-1-60973-134-2 (library reinforced : alk. paper)
  1. National Football Conference—Juvenile literature.
2. Football—West (U.S.)—Juvenile literature. I. Title.
  GV950.7.L32 2011
  796.332'640973—dc22   2011007154

Printed in the United States of America
Mankato, MN
April 2012
PA02132

TABLE OF
CONTENTS

NFC
WEST

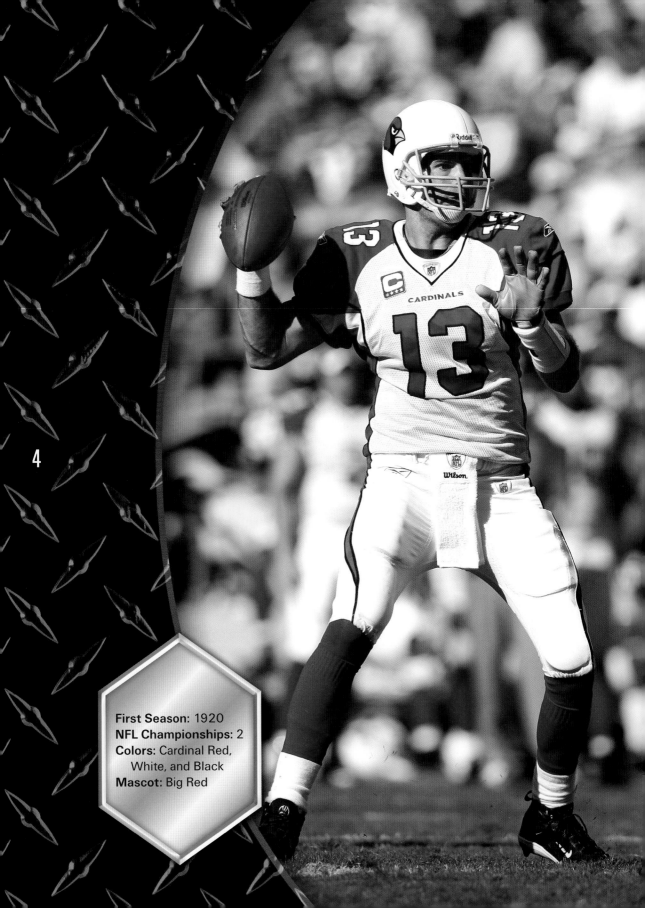

4

First Season: 1920
NFL Championships: 2
Colors: Cardinal Red,
White, and Black
Mascot: Big Red

★

ARIZONA
CARDINALS

FLYING FOREVER

The Cardinals have been playing football for more than 100 years. They started in Chicago as the Morgan Athletic Club in 1898. Then, in 1920, the Cardinals were one of the original 11 teams that formed the NFL. Although they have been around a long time, winning hasn't come easy. In fact, their only NFL championship titles came in 1925 and 1947!

The last couple of seasons have been some of the best for Cardinals fans. In 2008 they won their first NFC championship and played in their first Super Bowl. They fell to the Pittsburgh Steelers 27–23.

Now playing for the Cardinals, Kurt Warner was named MVP of Super Bowl XXXIV when he led the St. Louis Rams to victory.

HOME FIELD

The Cardinals play their home games at the University of Phoenix Stadium in Glendale, Arizona. It sits right next door to the home arena of the pro hockey team the Phoenix Coyotes. The stadium also plays host to the Fiesta Bowl, a college football bowl game.

BIG DAYS

★ The Cardinals have been flying high the past two seasons. In 2008, behind the stellar play of quarterback Kurt Warner, they made it to the Super Bowl for the first time in team history. They lost to the Pittsburgh Steelers.
★ In 2009 the Cardinals had their first 10-win season (10–6) since 1976. They beat the Green Bay Packers 51–45 in the wild card playoffs before falling to the New Orleans Saints 45–14. The Saints went on to win the Super Bowl.

University of Phoenix Stadium holds 63,400 fans during regular games, but can expand to seat 73,000 during bigger games such as the Super Bowl.

SUPERSTARS!

THEN

Dick (Night Train) Lane, cornerback: set NFL **interception**
record as a rookie
Pat Tillman, safety: aggressive tackler; left the NFL to serve in the
U.S. Army and died in combat
Kurt Warner, quarterback: led Arizona to their first-ever Super Bowl berth

NOW

Steve Breaston, return specialist: a touchdown threat on
kick and punt returns
Larry Fitzgerald, wide receiver: has the best set of hands in the league
Joey Porter, linebacker: four-time Pro Bowler called the
"toughest player in the NFL" by *Sports Illustrated*

★

STAT LEADERS

(All-time team leaders*)
Passing Yards: Jim Hart, 34,639
Rushing Yards: Ottis Anderson, 7,999
Receiving Yards: Roy Green, 8,497
Touchdowns: Roy Green, 70
Interceptions: Larry Wilson, 52

(*Through 2010 season.)

TIMELINE

1920
Chicago Cardinals become charter members of the NFL.

1947
Cardinals win the NFL championship, defeating the Philadelphia Eagles, 28–21; they also won in 1925.

1960
Cardinals move from Chicago to St. Louis, Missouri.

Wide receiver Larry Fitzgerald has been selected to the Pro Bowl in five of his seven NFL seasons.

1976
Cardinals capture the East Division title with a 10-4 regular season record.

1988
Cardinals move from St. Louis to Arizona.

2008
Cardinals appear in their first-ever Super Bowl, falling to the Pittsburgh Steelers 27–23.

First Season: 1946
NFL Championships: 5
Colors: Scarlet and Gold
Mascot: Sourdough
Sam

★

SAN FRANCISCO
49ERS

SUPER SAN FRANCISCO

The San Francisco 49ers are one of the greatest **dynasties** in football. They are the only team in the NFL to have played in five Super Bowl games *and* won all five. Starting in the late 1980s, they won 10 or more games 16 seasons in a row.

The Niners were led by some of the best players who ever stepped onto a field. Quarterback Joe Montana led San Francisco to four of the five Super Bowl titles and was named Super Bowl MVP three times. His favorite receiver, Jerry Rice, holds the NFL record for most touchdowns (208).

Running back Frank Gore is the first Niner ever to have four 1,000-yard seasons in a row.

HOME FIELD

The Niners play their home games in Candlestick Park, right near the San Francisco Bay. Winds from the water often swirl into the stadium and create wild and windy playing conditions. "The Stick" was built for the pro baseball team, the San Francisco Giants, but they moved out in 2000.

BIG DAYS

★ The 1988 Super Bowl between the Niners and the Cincinnati Bengals is one of the most memorable comebacks ever. The Niners were down 16–13, with just more than three minutes to go. They marched 92 yards down the field to score the winning touchdown with 35 seconds left in the game. The final score was 20–16.

★ In 1994, the 49ers became the first NFL team to win five Super Bowl titles. They rolled over the San Diego Chargers 49–26. San Francisco quarterback Steve Young threw a Super Bowl–record six touchdown passes.

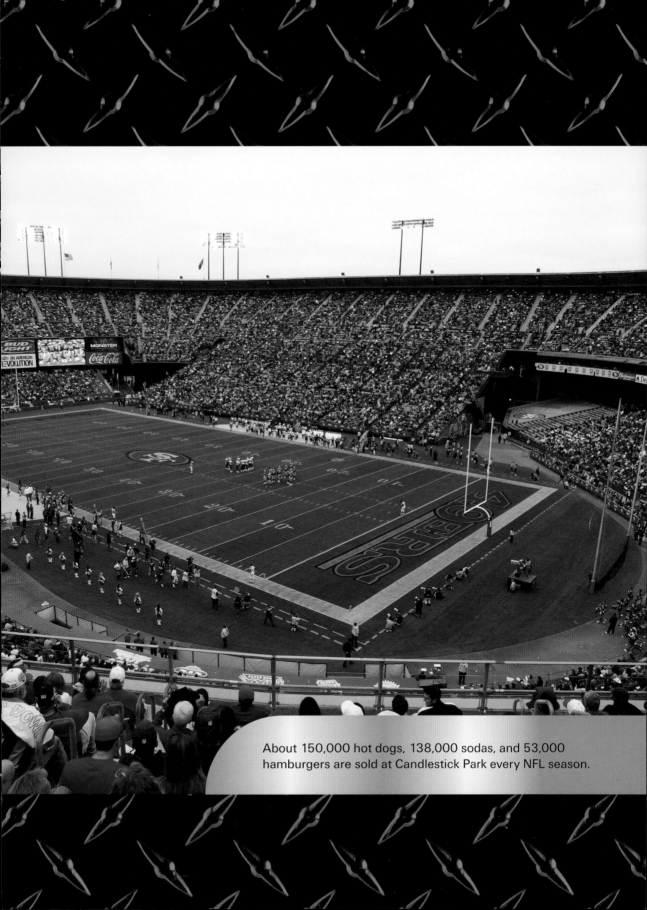

About 150,000 hot dogs, 138,000 sodas, and 53,000 hamburgers are sold at Candlestick Park every NFL season.

SUPERSTARS!

THEN

Ronnie Lott, cornerback and safety: earned All-Pro honors at three different positions

Joe Montana, quarterback: four-time Super Bowl MVP, "Joe Cool" was the master of come-from-behind victories

Jerry Rice, wide receiver: led the NFL in receiving yards and touchdown catches six times

NOW

Frank Gore, running back: named to two Pro Bowl teams

Justin Smith, defensive end: a two-time Pro Bowler, he led the team with 8.5 sacks in 2010

Patrick Willis, linebacker: led the NFL in tackles in 2008 and 2009

STAT LEADERS

(All-time team leaders*)

Passing Yards: Joe Montana, 35,124

Rushing Yards: Joe Perry, 7,344

Receiving Yards: Jerry Rice, 19,247

Touchdowns: Jerry Rice, 187

Interceptions: Ronnie Lott, 51

★

TIMELINE

(*Through 2010 season.)

1946	1950	1970	1971	1972	1981
San Francisco 49ers join the All-American Football Conference.	The Niners join the NFL.	San Francisco finishes 10–3–1 and wins its first division title in the Super Bowl **era.**	The Niners win their second NFC West title.	San Francisco wins a third NFC West title.	San Francisco wins the first of five Super Bowl titles, defeating the Cincinnati Bengals 26–21.

Linebacker Patrick Willis was named NFL Defensive Rookie of the Year in 2007.

1984

The Niners defeat the Miami Dolphins 38–16 in Super Bowl XIX; quarterback Joe Montana wins his second Super Bowl MVP Award.

1988

San Francisco defeats the Bengals again in the Super Bowl to win its third title.

1989

The 49ers defeat the Denver Broncos 55–10 for their fourth title in one of the most lopsided Super Bowl victories ever.

1994

San Francisco defeats the San Diego Chargers 49–26 to become the first team to win five Super Bowl titles.

First Season: 1976
NFL Championships: 0
Colors: Light Blue, Steel Blue, Neon Green, and White
Mascot: Blitz

★

SEATTLE
SEAHAWKS

SUPER IN SEATTLE

The Seattle Seahawks are one of the youngest teams in the NFL. They joined the league as an **expansion team** in the NFC in 1976. They are also the only team in the league to have played in both the American Football Conference (AFC) and the NFC. They switched to the AFC after just one season and then switched back to the NFC in 2002.

The Seahawks have made it to the Super Bowl once in their 34-year history. They lost to the Pittsburgh Steelers in the 2005 Super Bowl 21–10.

Quarterback Matt Hasselbeck is the highest-rated passer in Seahawks history.

HOME FIELD

The Seahawks play their home games in a multipurpose stadium called Qwest Field. In addition to the Seahawks, the Seattle Sounders, a professional soccer team, also play there.

BIG DAYS

★ Seattle won two division titles when they were still in the AFC (1988, 1999). Both times they finished with a 9–7 record and were knocked out in the first game of the playoffs.
★ Seattle has dominated the NFC West since joining in 2002. They have won four division titles (2004–2007) and won the NFC championship in 2005 after defeating the Carolina Panthers 15–3.

The 72,000-seat Qwest Field is located in Seattle, Washington.

SUPERSTARS!

THEN

Shaun Alexander, running back: named MVP of the league in 2005
Dave Krieg, quarterback: ranks in the all-time top 15 in most NFL passing categories
Steve Largent, wide receiver: led the NFL in receiving for two seasons and was named to the Pro Bowl seven times

NOW

Matt Hasselbeck, quarterback: smart, accurate, and experienced QB
Lawyer Milloy, safety: has made more than 20 **sacks** and 25 interceptions in his career
Leon Washington, running back: a return specialist, and one of the fastest in the league

STAT LEADERS

(All-time team leaders*)
Passing Yards: Matt Hasselbeck, 29,579
Rushing Yards: Shaun Alexander, 9,429
Receiving Yards: Steve Largent, 13,089
Touchdowns: Shaun Alexander, 112
Interceptions: Dave Brown, 50

(*Through 2010 season.)

TIMELINE

1976
Seattle joins the NFL in the NFC.

1977
Seahawks switch to the AFC.

1983
Seahawks make it to the playoffs for the first time in team history; they lose to the Los Angeles Raiders in the AFC championship 30-14.

1988
They win their first AFC West Division title.

1999
Seattle wins their second AFC West Division title.

Running back Shaun Alexander played eight seasons with the Seahawks before joining the Redskins for his final season in 2008.

2002	**2004**	**2005**	**2005**	**2007**
Seahawks switch to the NFC West Division.	They win their first of four NFC West Division titles.	The team finishes 13-3, their best record in franchise history.	Seattle plays in its first and only Super Bowl, falling to the Pittsburgh Steelers 21-10.	Seahawks win their fourth NFC West Division title in as many years.

First Season: 1936
NFL Championships: 3
Colors: Millennium Blue,
New Century Gold,
and White
Mascot: Rampage

★

ST. LOUIS
RAMS

ROOTING FOR THE RAMS

The Rams have played in three different cities and won a title in all three places. They won their first NFL title as the Cleveland Rams in 1945 when they defeated the Washington Redskins 15–14. They won as the Los Angeles Rams in 1951, defeating the Cleveland Browns 24–17. And they won the Super Bowl as the St. Louis Rams in 1999, defeating the Tennessee Titans 23–16.

The Rams have had some rough seasons in the past 10 years. In fact, they haven't had a winning one since 2003. But star quarterback Sam Bradford, a rookie in 2010, is the great hope to turn the franchise around.

Linebacker James Laurinaitis led the Rams in tackles for each of his first two seasons.

HOME FIELD

The Rams play their home games at the Edward Jones Dome in St. Louis. The Dome was built to lure an NFL team back to St. Louis. They had lost the Cardinals in 1987. The plan worked. The Rams moved from Los Angeles in early 1995.

BIG DAYS

★ The Los Angeles Rams were one of the best teams in the NFL from 1949 to 1955. They played in the NFL championship game four times and won one title (1951).

★ The Rams were known as the Greatest Show on Turf from 2000 to 2005. They racked up points behind the strong-armed quarterback Kurt Warner. Warner led them to two Super Bowls in 1999 and 2001. They beat the Tennessee Titans 23–16 in the first one but fell to the New England Patriots in the second, 20–17.

The 66,000-seat Edward Jones Dome has two video screens that are each 26 feet wide and 20 feet high.

SUPERSTARS!

★

THEN

Eric Dickerson, running back: ran for more than 1,800 yards in three of his first four seasons

Deacon Jones, defensive end: played in eight Pro Bowls

Kurt Warner, quarterback: won two NFL MVP Awards (1999 and 2001) and one Super Bowl MVP (1999)

★

NOW

Sam Bradford, quarterback: a rookie in 2010 with a strong arm and a football-smart mind

Steven Jackson, running back: rushed for more than 1,000 yards in five of his first six seasons

James Laurinaitis, linebacker: led the team in tackles as a rookie in 2009

★

STAT LEADERS

(All-time team leaders*)

Passing Yards: Jim Everett, 23,758

Rushing Yards: Steven Jackson, 7,948

Receiving Yards: Isaac Bruce, 14,109

Touchdowns: Marshall Faulk, 85

★

(*Through 2010 season.)

TIMELINE

1936
The Cleveland Rams form.

1945
Rams win their first NFL championship, defeating the Washington Redskins 15-14; it was their last game before moving to Los Angeles.

1946
Team moves to California to become the Los Angeles Rams.

1951
Rams defeat the Cleveland Browns 24-17 for their second NFL title.

In the 2010 season, rookie quarterback Sam Bradford took every one of the Rams' 1,053 offensive snaps.

1979
Los Angeles loses to the Pittsburgh Steelers in the Super Bowl 31–19.

1995
Team relocates to Missouri to become the St. Louis Rams.

1999
St. Louis wins Super Bowl title, defeating the Tennessee Titans 23–16; quarterback Kurt Warner is named MVP.

2001
Rams play in their second Super Bowl in three years but lose to the New England Patriots 20–17.

STAT
STUFF

★

NFC WEST DIVISION STATISTICS*

Team	All-Time Record (W-L-T)	NFL Titles (Most Recent)	Times in NFL Playoffs
Arizona Cardinals	483–680–39	1 (1947)	8
San Francisco 49ers	509–420–15	5 (1994)	23
Seattle Seahawks	256–275–0	0	11
St. Louis Rams	510–492–20	3 (1999)	27

★

NFC WEST DIVISION CHAMPIONSHIPS
(MOST RECENT)

Arizona Cardinals . . . 2 (2009)

San Francisco 49ers . . . 17 (2002)

Seattle Seahawks . . . 5 (2010)

St. Louis Rams . . . 11 (2003)

★

(*Through 2010 season.)

Position Key:
QB: Quarterback
RB: Running back
WR: Wide receive
T: Tackle
G: Guard
CB: Cornerback
LB: Linebacker
DE: Defensive end
HB: Halfback
S: Safety
FB: Fullback
DT: Defensive tacl
TE: Tight end

NFC WEST PRO FOOTBALL HALL OF FAME MEMBERS

Arizona Cardinals

Charles W. Bidwill Sr., Owner, Administrator
Jimmy Conzelman, QB, Coach, Owner
Dan Dierdorf, T
John (Paddy) Driscoll, QB
Walt Kiesling, G, Coach
Dick "Night Train" Lane, CB
Ollie Matson, HB
Ernie Nevers, FB
Jackie Smith, TE
Charley Trippi, HB, QB
Roger Wehrli, CB
Larry Wilson, S

San Francisco 49ers

Fred Dean, DE
Jimmy Johnson, CB
John Henry Johnson, FB
Ronnie Lott, CB, S
Hugh McElhenny, HB
Joe Montana, QB
Leo Nomellini, DT
Joe Perry, FB
Jerry Rice, WR
Bob St. Clair, T
Y. A. Tittle, QB
Bill Walsh, Coach
Dave Wilcox, LB
Steve Young, QB

Seattle Seahawks

Steve Largent, WR
John Randle, DT

St. Louis Rams

George Allen, Coach
Eric Dickerson, RB
Tom Fears, DE
Sid Gillman, Coach
Marshall Faulk, RB
Elroy "Crazylegs" Hirsch, HB
David "Deacon" Jones, DE
Tom Mack, G
Ollie Matson, HB
Merlin Olsen, DT
Dan Reeves, Owner, Administrator
Andy Robustelli, DE
Les Richter, LB
Tex Schramm, Administrator
Jackie Slater, T
Norm Van Brocklin, QB
Bob Waterfield, QB
Jack Youngblood, DE

NOTE: Includes players with at least three seasons with the team. Players may appear with more than one team.

GLOSSARY

★

dynasties (DYE-nuh-steez): teams that dominate their sport for an extended period of time

era (EER-uh): a period of time marked by a certain event

expansion team (ek-SPAN-shuhn TEEM): a club added to a league that makes the league bigger

franchise (FRAN-chize): the right or license of a team to call itself a certain name

interception (in-tur-SEPT-shun): the act of a defensive player catching a pass intended for an offensive player

sacks (SAKS): tackling the quarterback behind the line of scrimmage before he throws the ball

FIND OUT MORE

★

BOOKS

Buckley, James, Jr. *Scholastic Ultimate Guide to Football*.
New York: Franklin Watts, 2009.

MacRae, Sloan. *The San Francisco 49ers*.
New York: PowerKids Press, 2011.

Stewart, Mark. *The Arizona Cardinals*. Chicago:
Norwood House Press, 2009.

Stewart, Mark. *The Seattle Seahawks*. Chicago:
Norwood House Press, 2009.

Stewart, Mark. *The St. Louis Rams*. Chicago:
Norwood House Press, 2009.

★

WEB SITES

For links to learn more about football visit
www.childsworld.com/links

Note to Parents, Teachers, and Librarians: We routinely verify our Web links to make sure
they are safe and active sites. So encourage your readers to check them out!

INDEX

ABOUT THE AUTHOR

Ellen Labrecque has written many books for young readers on football, basketball, baseball, and other sports. Labrecque was an editor for *Sports Illustrated Kids*. She loves to watch her Philadelphia Eagles.